Christmas Wishes
FROM THE HEART

Ribbons of Love

Christmas Wishes

Gardens of Friendship

Happy Is the House: That Shelters a Friend

In the Presence of Angels

Just for You

Loving Thoughts

Mother: Another Word for Love

Christmas Wishes

Brownlow

BROWNLOW PUBLISHING COMPANY, INC.

Welcome Merry Christmas

Be merry all, be merry all,

With holly dress the festive hall;

Prepare the song, the feast, the ball,

To welcome merry Christmas.

W. R. SPENCER

As Candles Glow

The candles glow
on Christmas branches;
How brightly shines
our Christmas tree!
Each tiny light speaks to
us of heaven,
Of heaven's hope given
you and me.

With merry hearts all the
children gather.
Their eyes are laughing,
their faces gay,
And older hearts sing a
song of gladness
To praise the Lord for this
happy day.

INGEBORG STOLEE

A Victorian Christmas

A busy time is the English Christmas. The keynote of the jollity and genuine happiness is that everyone loves his neighbor more than himself. "Peace and goodwill" is the British Christmas slogan. The atmosphere is so full of the golden rule that if Mrs. Upper Crust meets Mrs. O'Toole who takes in washing, they both greet each other with "Merry Christmas" though the next day Mrs. Upper Crust passes Mrs. O'Toole by with a dignified bow, which is returned in like manner by Mrs. O'Toole, who knows her place.

Christmas began in the heart of God.

It is complete only when it reaches the heart of man.

Christmas is the day
that holds all time
together.

ALEXANDER SMITH

Christmas Wishes From a Friend

Now may joy-bells in your heart
Ring full merrily, my friend.
Many a joyous Christmas wish
With this greeting do I send.
Pray accept them, friend of mine—
From a friendly heart sincere.
Friendship should the brighter shine
When the Christmas-tide is here.

MARY D. BRINE

Christmas Tonight

Everywhere—everywhere, Christmas tonight!

Christmas in lands of the Fir tree and Pine,

Christmas in lands of the Palm tree and vine,

Christmas where snow peaks stand

solemn and white,

Christmas where corn fields lie

sunny and bright,

Everywhere, everywhere, Christmas tonight.

PHILLIPS BROOKS

Christmas Bells

*H*ark! the
Christmas bells are ringing—
Ringing through the frosty air—
Happiness to each one bringing,
And release from toil and care.

How the merry peal is swelling
From the gray old crumbling tower,
To the simplest creature telling
Of Almighty love and power.

Ankle-deep the snow is lying;
Every spray is clothed in white.
Now around the folk are waving,
Brisk and busy, gay and light.

Neighbors shaking hands and greeting,
No one sorrowing, no one sad,
Children, loving parents meeting,
Young and old alike are glad.

Then while Christmas bells are ringing,
Rich and poor, your voices raise,
And—your simple carol singing—
Waft to heaven your grateful praise.

The Snowman

Our snowman, our snowman,
We've built him up in haste;
We knew not when the frost might break,
We had no time to waste;
So first we gathered up the snow
And piled it in a heap;
For melons, ice, and snowmen
Are things that will not keep.

A Christmas Carol

The Christ-child lay on Mary's lap,
    His hair was like a light.
(O weary, weary were the world,
    But here is all aright.)

The Christ-child lay on Mary's breast,
    His hair was like a star.
(O stern and cunning are the kings,
    But here the true hearts are.)

The Christ-child lay on Mary's heart,
　　His hair was like a fire.
(O weary, weary is the world,
　　But here the world's desire.)

The Christ-child stood at Mary's knee,
　　His hair was like a crown.
And all the flowers looked up at him,
　　And all the stars looked down.

G. K. CHESTERTON

Christmas Friends

These holly leaves to you I send

To bear my Christmas greeting

And say our friendship ne'er shall end

Though life itself be fleeting.

VIRGINIA B. HARRISON

The Night the Angels Sang

And there were shepherds living out in the fields nearby, keeping watch over their flocks at night. An angel of the Lord appeared to them, and the glory of the Lord shone around them, and they were terrified. But the angel said to them,

"Do not be afraid. I bring you good news of great joy that will be for all the people. Today in the town of David a Savior has been born to you; he is Christ the Lord. This will be a sign to you: You will find a baby wrapped in cloths and lying in a manger."

Suddenly a great company of the heavenly host appeared with the angel, praising God and saying,

"Glory to God in the highest,
   and on earth peace to men on
      whom his favor rests."

When the angels had left them and gone into heaven, the shepherds said to one another,

"Let's go to Bethlehem and see this thing that has happened, which the Lord has told us about."

So they hurried off and found Mary
and Joseph, and the baby, who was lying in
the manger. When they had seen him, they
spread the word concerning what had been
told them about this child, and all who heard
it were amazed at what the shepherds said to
them. But Mary treasured up all these things
and pondered them in her heart. The shepherds
returned, glorifying and praising God for all
the things they had heard and seen, which
were just as they had been told.

LUKE 2:8-20

Very happy may it be

Christmastime

to thine and thee.

CHRISTMAS CARD, 1884

What sweeter music

can we bring

Than carol for to sing.

A Victorian Christmas

The Christmas spirit starts at least a week before the actual day. Young girls and their admirers take possession of the kitchen in the evenings and occupy themselves for at least two hours, getting ready the plum puddings to be distributed among the poor.

The girls stone the raisins and pick over the currants while the boys chop the suet and cut into thin slices the tough citron peel. Occasionally one or other bursts out into caroling.

Then, at about ten o'clock in the evening, the Queen of the Kitchen (the cook) arrives and takes possession while the young people wash their sticky hands.

The cook in England is such an absolute monarch that at her word all scatter away. The night's work is completed by serving steaming hot chocolate. Next evening, after preparations for the puddings are complete, the boys beat the eggs and are given the work of stirring the contents. Each of the party has to give a stir, for that brings luck to the stirrers. Then comes the long evening, when these precious puddings are put in their respective cloths, looking like huge puffballs before they are dropped into the copper of boiling water. The boys take turns as stokers, for there is no convenient gas stove under the copper. The Christmas songs and carols are sung, and stories told, until Kitchen Queen announces that the puddings "have biled long enough and it's time you young ladies and gents got out of *my* kitchen."

Songs
of Cherubs

Hark! the carol heavenward floats;

Listen to the liquid notes:

Listen well and you may hear

Songs of cherubs hovering near.

EUGENE FIELD

Are You Ready for Christmas?

Are you willing to stoop down and consider the needs and desires of little children; to remember the weaknesses and loneliness of people who are growing old; to stop asking how much your friends love you, and to ask yourself whether you love them enough; to bear in mind the things that other people have to bear on their hearts; to trim your lamp so that it will give more light and less smoke, and to carry it in front so that your shadow will fall behind you; to make a grave for your ugly thoughts and a garden for your kindly feelings, with the gate open? Are you willing to do these things for a day? Then you are ready to keep Christmas!

HENRY VAN DYKE

I Think of You

Take from my heart,

though not my hand,

A wish that you will understand,

A greeting that is kind and true,

Because it means I think of you.

C. B.

Angels
We Have Heard
on High

Angels we have heard on high
Sweetly singing o'er the plains
And the mountains in reply,
Echoing their joyous strains.

Shepherds, why this jubilee?
Why your joyous songs prolong?
What the gladsome tidings be
Which inspire your heav'nly song?

Come to Bethlehem and see
Him whose birth the angels sing;
Come, adore on bended knee,
Christ the Lord, the newborn King.

Christmas Greetings

Christmas greetings fond and true,

This is what I wish for you.

"Merry Christmas!" May the day

Bring you all that's bright and gay.

Christmas-tide should bring good cheer.

All of that be with you, dear.

MARY D. BRINE

A Victorian Christmas

Before Christmas Eve arrives the morning is spent beautifying the churches. Holly berries are underfoot, the young men doing the ladder work, with the girls beneath saying in anxious tones, "Oh, do be careful. You might fall."

Then Christmas evening—*the mystery of it!* Parcels are done up with their bright wrappings and ribbons. The tree in the dining room is decorated and the hallway adorned with holly and mistletoe. Sly chaps are hanging a sprig of mistletoe over each doorway so that the girls will have no chance to escape a kiss, even if they want to.

The yule log is brought in and placed on the great fireplace. It is considered good luck if each member of the family in turn sits upon the log and salutes it before it is lighted. According to custom, bad luck will reign in the household if the entire log is consumed on Christmas Eve, for some of the embers and pieces should be saved to start the New Year's Eve fire.

At eleven o'clock in the evening, the call comes to prepare for church and the young folks calm down, for England's religious life is taken seriously and any frivolity at that time would place a black mark against a culprit's future welcome. There are carols and Christmas hymns joined in by all (young and old—sweet young voices and voices that are old and quavery), and the whole atmosphere is filled with homage paid to the memory of the wonderful Babe. As the worshipers pass out of the church, bells ring out all over the towns and merry greetings begin.

Merry Christmas Morning

A Merry Christmas morning

To each and every one!

The rose has kissed the dawning

And the gold is in the sun.

And may the Christmas splendor

A joyous greeting bear

Of love that's true and tender

And faith that's sweet and fair!

Why do the bells of Christmas ring?
Why do little children sing?

Once a lovely, shining star,
Seen by shepherds from afar,
Gently moved until its light
Made a manger's cradle bright.

There a darling baby lay,
Pillowed soft upon the hay;
And its mother sung and smiled,
"This is Christ, the holy child!"

Therefore bells for Christmas ring,
Therefore little children sing.

EUGENE FIELD

A Victorian Christmas

The Victorians resurrected the old English custom of singing Christmas carols, and they composed many new ones we now treasure. After church on Christmas Eve, parties of carol singers come to the front of the houses with a wagon drawn by a stalwart horse. On the wagon is always an ancient *harmonium*, or American organ, and someone plays for the others to sing.

When the householders are beloved there is the lovely song "God Bless the Master of This House." A silver offering exchanges hands, and in many houses hot coffee is ready and cake in goodly quantity to "warm their whistles," as they express it.

Christmas Carol

Burn, Christmas lights,

burn chaste and clear!

Blaze out against the stormy sky

From windows warm

with Christmas cheer

And rosy tapers flaming high!

All sparkling, glowing greetings send,

From lip of love and heart of friend,

And bear to those who grieve alone

Glad tidings sent to every one.

Peal, Christmas bells,

peal loud and deep!

Ring out a merry Christmas chime

Till darkened eyes forebear to weep

And hard hearts glow with love divine;

In rippling music die away,

With ringing laughter glad and gay,

Till rich and full the dark night swells

With Christmas lights

and Christmas bells!

ELAINE GOODALE

The hinge of history

is on the door

of a Bethlehem stable.

RALPH W. SOCKMAN

Christmas turns all wise souls from the surface which is time to the center which is eternity.

E. MERRILL ROOT

A Victorian Christmas

*A*t eight o'clock Christmas morning there is a meeting of the younger members of the family and their friends—all clad in a

miscellaneous and motley lot of dressing gowns—
and amid giggles they creep to the door of the
hosts of the house. After sundry false starts,
owing to pitching the notes too high or too low,
they burst forth into "Hark, the Herald Angels
Sing!" Then they tiptoe mysteriously away, so
when the door is opened to show appreciation,
no one is visible and the master and mistress
of the house are supposed to stretch their

imaginations to think it really was the "angels."

Next they meet in the dining room and seem astonished to find it decorated and a Christmas tree there in all its beauty, covered and banked up with presents. No one is forgotten, for the servants all come in for their gifts too.

The Christmas tree is now in every home

as the focal point of the seasonal decorations. Queen Victoria's husband, Prince Albert, is given credit for establishing the tree custom in England when he imported German trees in 1841. In reality Queen Charlotte, wife of George III, had decorated a tree in Windsor Castle many years earlier.

Christmas Tea

When you and your dollies

so festive and jolly

Sit down to your Christmas tea,

Since I can't come tripping

to join your sipping

Please drink a wee cupful for me.

NINETEENTH-CENTURY CHRISTMAS CARD

Christmastide

O'er the earth in wondrous beauty pealing
  Ring again the happy Christmas bells;
Into every heart sweet peace is stealing,
  Wakened by the joy that in them dwells.

To the souls of all who hear them ringing,
  Comes the thought of that first Christmas time,

When above the hills of Judah singing
  Angel voices chanted notes sublime.

Far away the simple shepherds hear them,
  And behold the gleaming, radiant star;
While upon their way the Magi journey,
  Bringing precious offerings from afar.

To the Holy Babe within the manger,
  Sheltered by the Virgin's tender love,

Guarded safe from every harm and danger
By his Father's power in heaven above.

Through the ages that are past and ended,
Comes the joy of that first Christmas time.
O'er the earth in all its radiant splendor
Shines that star, illumining every clime.

MARY C. SHAFER

Now Christmas is come,

Let's beat up the drum,

And call all our neighbors together,

And when they appear,

Let us make them such cheer

As will keep out the wind and the weather.

WASHINGTON IRVING

Holy Night

As Doctor Stevens came into the village

He let his horse slow down to a walk.

The moon broke through the clouds.

There was not a track on the new-fallen snow.

He was thinking how nice it was

That the Judson baby had come on Christmas Eve.

He smiled his pleasant smile

As he passed lighted houses with trimmed trees inside.

What could Ellen Hicks be doing up at this late hour?

She didn't have anyone to be filling stockings for.

Poor thing! She didn't have anything to fill a stocking with.

A shadow moved regularly across the drawn shade.

She was sitting there rocking—rocking.

The village clock struck eleven.

From the south came the faint tinkle of sleigh bells.

The snow creaked as he went up the steps.

The rocking stopped.

The light moved through the door into the hall.

Ellen unlocked the door.

She held the light up to see who her late caller was.
She had a worn patchwork quilt around her shoulders.
The doctor went over to the chunk stove to warm his hands.
It gave out no heat. He touched it. It was barely warm.
No, of course there wasn't anything the matter with her.

She always sat up until midnight on Christmas Eve.
She'd got to thinking about that Stebbins family,
And sat there rocking and forgot her fire.
How they could get along with all those young ones,
And him all crippled, she couldn't see.

They didn't even have wood to keep them warm.

"Ellen, have you been giving wood to the Stebbinses?"

She admitted she had called the boy in and loaded his sled.

Well, maybe she *had* sent some food.

Little by little the truth came out.

Her nephew did look after her; he always had.

But he'd told her she'd got to stop this sharing.

She'd promised.

But she couldn't bear to think of those Stebbinses.

She could get along. She still had wood in the shed.

The doctor's scolding stuck in his throat.

He went to the shed and brought in the last armful of wood.

He shut the stable door.

He stopped to look down on the sleeping village.

So Ellen had to share. He recalled the look on her face.

Sharing. That was what Christmas meant.

The clock in the village struck twelve.

Down in the valley a rooster crowed.

Overhead the moon moved slowly across the winter sky.

Holy night. Peaceful night.

WALTER HARD

The All of Christmas

God grant you the light in Christmas,
which is faith; the warmth of Christmas,
which is love; the radiance of Christmas,
which is purity; the righteousness
of Christmas, which is justice;
the belief in Christmas, which is truth;
the *all* of Christmas, which is Christ.

WILDA ENGLISH

Old-Time Christmas

Just the old-time Christmas greeting,

Just the same great wish I send;

Just the same old message, speaking

Love that loves unto the end.

MARY C. LOW

Christmas Is Coming

Christmas is coming,

the geese are getting fat.

Please to put a penny in an old man's hat.

If you haven't got a penny,

a ha'penny will do.

If you haven't got a ha'penny, God bless you.

The Christmas Spirit

I am the Christmas spirit!

I enter the home of poverty, causing pale-faced children to open their eyes wide in pleased wonder.

I cause the miser's clutched hand to relax, and thus paint a bright spot on his soul.

I cause the aged to renew their youth and to laugh in the old, glad way.

I keep romance alive in the heart of childhood, and brighten sleep with dreams woven of magic.

I cause eager feet to climb dark stairways with filled baskets, leaving behind hearts amazed at the goodness of the world.

I cause the prodigal to pause a moment on his wild, wasteful way, and send to anxious love some little token that releases glad tears—tears which wash away the hard lines of sorrow.

I enter dark prison cells, reminding scarred manhood of what might have been, and pointing forward to good days yet to be.

I come softly into the still, quiet home of pain, and lips that are too weak to speak just tremble in silent, eloquent gratitude.

In a thousand ways I cause the weary world to look up into the face of God, and for a little moment forget the things that are small and wretched.

I am the Christmas spirit!

E. C. Baird

The Adoration of the Wise Men

Saw you never in the twilight,
While the sun had left the skies,
Up in heaven the clear stars shining
Through the gloom like silver eyes?
So of old the wise men watching
Saw a little stranger star,
And they knew the King was given,
And they follow'd it from far.

Heard you never of the story,
How they cross'd the desert wild,
Journey'd on by plain and mountain,
Till they found the Holy Child?

How they open'd all their treasure,
Kneeling to that Infant King,
Gave the gold and fragrant incense,
Gave the myrrh in offering?

Know ye not that lowly Baby
Was the bright and morning star,
He who came to light the Gentiles
And the darken'd isles afar?

And we too may seek His cradle,
There our heart's best treasures bring,
Love, and Faith, and true devotion,
For our Saviour, God, and King.

CECIL FRANCES ALEXANDER

A Victorian Christmas

Christmas dinner is usually served at either half-past one in the afternoon or half-past seven in the evening. Either way, it is a feast to be remembered throughout the year. Roast beef is the traditional favorite in northern England, while they prefer goose in the South. As times become more prosperous, turkey is popular.

If dinner is served in the afternoon, the old folks follow it with a rest while the young ones go for a brisk walk or, if there is ice, enjoy skating.

The evening meal consists of the remainders from dinner and a blazing plum pudding.

*It is
Christmas
in the heart that
puts Christmas
in the air.*

Christmas Eve

'Tis Christmas Eve.

The twilight creepeth stilly

To hush with restful calm the busy day;

O'er snow-lapt fields the darkness gathers chilly,

And slowly fades the sunset's

paling ray.

Hushed is the

household's varying commotion,

And silently about the fire we sit;

Loosed is the tension of a strained emotion,

The cord of life with which our hearts are knit.

The flickering firelight, and the shadows falling,

We follow with unconscious,

dreamy gaze,

The living

present lost in dim recalling

The joys or sorrows of our bygone days.

'Tis Christmas Eve! A sacred peace is stealing

Upon the aching heart and weary brain,

An undefined, a sweet and holy feeling

Stills the quick throbbing

of a restless pain.—

We lost Thee

in the hour of dark temptation,

Forgot to look for succor from above—

We find Thee, O our heart's Divine Salvation!

Bring Thy sweet messages

of peace and love!

ELAINE GOODALE

Then let the holly red be hung,

And all the sweetest carols sung,

While we with joy remember them—

The journeyers to Bethlehem.

FRANK DEMPSTER SHERMAN